HITCH YOUR HEART

Come Sail 'Again' *with* Me
through Mind Hitching
Poetry *and* Prose

May F. Lindsey Reed

First edition published 2015. Lucas Park Books edition published 2019. Poems copyright ©2015 by May F. Lindsey Reed.

All rights reserved. No part of this book may be reproduced or transmitted in any form or by any means without permission in writing from the copyright owner or his representative. For permission to reuse content, please email gwdmin@att.net.

ISBN: 978-1-60350-077-7

Published by Lucas Park books
www.lucasparkbooks.com

Printed in the United States of America

**Dedicated to my loving sister,
Loretta Lindsey**

**AND
ALL MY FRIENDS.**

And what would life be
without friends.

Jesus, my dearest, and most
precious, loving friend
has given me
all of you. ☺
I'm ever so humbled and grateful too
that this for me
He would do.

My love to everyone!
It is pure joy for me to
write these poems.☺

**A special remembrance of my darling friend
and brother in Christ,
Oscar Haynes,
former editor of The Oldtimers' GrapeVine.
At 98 years and with his gracious style
and contagious smile
he
journeyed Home to be with The Father,
1916–2014.
He will never be forgotten.
"UNFORGETTABLE, THAT'S WHAT YOUR ARE"**

TABLE OF CONTENTS

Foreword	viii
Preface	ix
Hitch Your Heart to the Morning Star	1
They Had A Moment	3
My Family's Lovin Chicken Fest	8
Firmament – Nature – Beauty	9
Enjoy Life's Nuts	11
Those Awful Nosebleeds (Non-fiction)	12
Keep Sparkling Pam and Family (Non-fiction)	14
John Richard Foulkes (Non-fiction)	16
An Incident: A Good Ending (Non-fiction)	18
Daily – Changes Come	19
Never Mind! Just Never Mind!	21
The Tie–Your Tie–My Tie	23
Chatter Box	24
Happy Recollections of My Childhood (Non-fiction)	25
I Only Wanted To Look At the Boat (Non-fiction)	32
I Don't Know (Non fiction)	34
I'm Salty	36
Tomorrow Comes Again and Again	37
End of Me Day (Non-fiction)	38
Tree, Squirrel, Chipmunk, and Me Too	40
He Made It Back Home	43

Where Have You Been In Your Day Dreams?	47
When We Only Had The Old Radio	49
William Kappan Fox (Non-fiction)	51
My Alameda Memories and Thoughts	53
A Christmas Party Indeed	54
It Can Be An Isthmus Christmas	56
Try Living Life HIS Way	58
A Blarney New Year It's About To Be – It Is	63
Famine or Feast of Life	65
The Isness of Life	66
The Child – A Wonder	67
We'll Give Them A Rose Garden (Non-fiction)	68
Time Is Fleeing: Only Nature Seeing	71
Quaff Deeply the Good Things of Life	72
Poetically Speaking	74
Things Will Be OK	76
Season of Joy	78
Cherisna (Non-fiction)	79
Dory, A Troubled Child	80
In My Heart	81
For Just A Few Moments: Rise Above It All.	82
Chobey and the Green Glass Eye	83
Clothed for Worship	84
This Morning's Prayer	86

Thoughts and Concerns	87
My Tribute to Billye Pinkston Bridges	88
Tomorrow Day	90
Little Whistler Boy	91
Beth and PUPPY	93
One Child's Prayer.	95
Led to Manhood	96
Sometimes It's Not the Words – But the View	97
Hallelujah! Christ Is Born	99
I Was Just Thinking	100
Shoo Bro. Blues	101
I Don't Need These	102
Prayerfully Shared Thoughts	103
Snowflake Ballet	104
LIFE! LIFE! LIFE?	106

FOREWORD

Often poetry is rather profound and you won't find the average individual reading from its pages. May's poetry will give her readers an uplift and energize the mind. Her words are illuminating, manifesting a genuine creativeness of what God has given which compels a need from within to share her gift with others.

May says, "HE has given me imagination, dreams, belief, and a tinge of moxie. I listen and meditate as I palaver (talk) with His Spirit. His Holy infinite messages come to me like music playing in my head – much like when I was a child for I'd hear every note as though the song was actually being played and would need no accompaniment to sing."

May's originality of poetry/prose will delight the Christian and every other reader. Her common sense touch brings life to her thoughts and words. Her non-fiction works, especially those referring to her childhood are utterly delightful.

PREFACE

When I was a little girl, words were magical to me; that is, words like "Once upon A Time." It seemed it must be a time and place far, far away and full of delightful characters as in a dream. And I would imagine all sorts of wonderful things whenever I read Fairy Tales, poems and tales of adventure.

"Once Upon A Time" I thought, must be a land in another world unlike anyplace I'd ever seen or ever would see. Somehow I came to know and under- stand that it is the magic in one's own mind —like that of the ancient writers which created the "Once Upon A Time" phrasing. I decided my own stories, poetry, tales that lived and grew in my own little special thought garden should be published and began to share my works with other writers/readers.

THE FRONT COVER also displays the cover of her First volume of poetry that was published in April of 2004, "Come Sail with Me into a Sea of Poetry."

VENUS is known both as the Evening Star and the Morning Star. Venus' highly reflective cloud cover and proximity to the earth makes it the brightest object in the universe other than the sun and moon. Venus is second nearest the Sun, seen in the eastern sky before or at sunrise. It is the only planet that rotates clockwise.

During eastern elongation it follows the Sun down at sunset and is then visible as an evening star. During western elongation it precedes the rising of the Sun

Why not hitch your heart to the Evening Star and rise, too, in that spectacular, gleaming, bursting radiance of sunbeams with the Morning Star.

HITCH YOUR HEART
TO THE MORNING STAR

Enjoy life! every day of it, in every way of it;
not just the things you love to do
but all those other things which
accompany it too.
When folk don't smile or talk to you
just smile anyway;
don't frown and rue.
When a look or a glance is of noticeable disdain,
don't let it worry, deflate, weight and drain.
Don't let it fill your heart with hurt, grief and pain.
Don't let it burden or cause despair.
Don't let it fill you with doubt, woe and care.
Why you can hitch your heart to the Morning Star.
Be content in your soul
with the way you are.

Just hitch your heart to the Morning Star.
Fill your mind with light,
and nothing good – bar....
Precede the sunshine with hope and elation,
removing heaviness, discontent,
weary frustration.
Oh, hitch your heart to the Morning Star;
receive life-giving energy from which
you'll never tire......
And our Morning Star is JESUS!

                                          Written Mon., March 21, 2005

PREFACE TO 'THEY HAD A MOMENT'

Marriage can be beautiful, sweet, and usually a
new bride or groom
is looking forward to a most wonderful
and exhilarating experience.
Someone to become as close to as their own
heartbeat.
Someone who will share and listen to their thoughts
and be tender,
and interested in their interests.
A love to embrace that embraces them.
When a young man or woman holds these hopes
and imagines their mate does too
but finds an ill nature that holds little
yielding to the warmth
and interests of their union
it can almost break their heart.
What they have studied, worked and struggled for;
earned, learned and prepared for their life
for which to provide their livelihood
but finding no cooperation within their mate
to support their labor for their home –
in time can become more than they can bear.
Moment after moment is rejected.
Moment after moment is lost.
Moment after moment is made hollow,
sometimes painful and empty.
But the moment may come when the one
can take no more and cannot return
again through that door.

The moment may come when they will walk
through that door one last time
and finding no
solace
are compelled to leave the burning fury behind.
but – 'They, the bitter one, had a moment'
indeed,
They had had many, many moments to change,
To receive.

THEY HAD A MOMENT

'They' had, in fact, a moment to be kind,
but 'They' were always tart, tense, sharp
and seldom gentle; uh-huh!
'They' didn't seem to be able to find the right
moment or the right way to
release their anger and just let-fly,
sharp, shrill and unkind words
but 'They' had a moment.
Their desire, it did seem, at every chance,
was a need to put the one down,
to give a jab of hostility and bitterness,
and would seem to be
just waiting for a retort that would send
them into a frenzy of loud, unkind words; yeah!
But 'They' had a moment.

The one sought peace and tranquility;
expressing their thoughts in moderate tones,
hesitating before speaking,
attempting to hold back what might cause
an emission of torrential emotions
but this seemed only to set the teeth
of the other and cause them to
be even more up-wroth.
The one sought a response of
calm but would sometimes have to actually
exit the home;
but 'They' had a moment.

When one accepts, unknowingly,
the pursuit of another or pursues someone
then finds there's a demon to deal with,

a demon within that is lacking the ability
to give or receive real love….
what shall they do?
There are those who want love desperately
or what they think is love
but when love comes
they're unable to
recognize it and struggle hard against
that love;
appearing never to have truly learned
how to give or receive love.
To them love is things – getting,
not giving
of themselves.
To them love is possessing
and demanding,
Wanting things according to
their terms.
The one must be at their beck and call,
their every whim.
If the one's opinion is asked,
the response is quickly rejected
for it never seems to be exactly what they
want to hear.
Oh yeah, 'They' had a moment.
And when the one is tired, exhausted,
and sometimes finds it difficult to sit and chat
at the close of day
and falls asleep,
oh what an angry fire is kindled.
Now on occasion when both are rested,
and energy-filled,

and the one asks the other
"Is there anything in particular you'd like to do?"
Too often the other can only angrily remember
the one disappointingly falling asleep
a few evenings prior and begins to
rehash their disappointment – rejecting and
refusing to receive this precious moment
which could be used for enjoyment,
fun, and happy laughter.
Yes, 'They' had a moment.
And this is the way most of the one's days
were made to be lived.

Occasionally the other would be
simply charming;
set a table so genteel,
smile ever so sweetly and make the one feel
love tranquil.
But let the one miss a single step
and ugly words are formed
and hurled.
Angry glances break the glow of the hour.
'They' appear unable to realize that the one is
there because of love for them,
wants to be loved
and would truly have to love
to be there at all
but 'They' again tear and shatter the moment.

The one keeps praying, hoping,
awaiting for that golden moment
but 'They' keep driving the one towards the door

and have again and again the love ignored.

Moments 'They' just wouldn't see.
Moments 'They' just couldn't see,
Didn't want to see.

Too busy rejecting, resisting,
and resenting each moment love presented itself
And lost what could have been
a happy and forever union.
Humph, 'They' had a moment,
many moments in fact.
'They'd' never learned to freely give
but mostly take.
'They' hadn't learned how to let a man
be a man –
how to tell him things he may need to know,
but in a way that didn't hurt, anger
embarrass or wound his soul.
Oh, why do some of us repeatedly
forfeit the moment?
Why do we throw away
the thing we want most....?
L O V E....
But 'They' had a moment....
Yes! Yes indeed,
'They' had a moment!
they had many, many moments.

Written March 7, 2002

MY FAMILY'S LOVIN CHICKEN FEST

Well Aunt Mabel set the table
and
Mama Shedd prepared the bread.
Sis. Mollie Dee brought her tasty, sweet tea
and
old Grandpa Dennis drank with glee.
The sun was bright, so high in the sky;
this was a blessed day
which money couldn't buy.
Mom's, Dad's and children laughed
and
talked up a storm –
the family Chicken Fest this year
was truly, newly reborn.
This little family of mine came together
each July.
The joy we generated this year
surely resounded in the courts on High.
They'd positioned me comfortably in a
large recliner chair.
They always fixed a place for me
that showed their love and care.
Since Vietnam I can no longer stand;
it was hard for me at first
but after nearly forty years
I've gotten through the worst.
Since God saw fit to let me live I'll just
praise His Holy Name,
for I've still got
my little Chicken Fest Family
and
a world of love to claim.

Written Thurs., October 13, 2005

FIRMAMENT – NATURE - BEAUTY

Much like sipping from an overflowing,
fragrant cup,
when I think of God's blessings from which
we frequent sup.
As we drove away from Charlotte, North Carolina,
one crisp, March morn –
mounds of fluffy, white, cotton candy clouds
hovered lazily, appearing pure and newly born;
virtually encapsulated within a soft shimmering,
powdery blue sky –
kissed by the sun's
dazzling brilliance which was a-blazing high.

The heaven's radiance spilled lavishly,
copiously like soft spun lace,
creating a spectacularly vivid luster of color
on all its view embraced.
The flowers, bushes, plants and trees,
complimenting one another under a calm,
gentle breeze;
growing side-by-side, betwixt enter-lacing roots –
intertwined together tis
grafting of shoots.

Earth never ceases to yield, wield;
bringing forth growth and beauty that excites the
eye and mind –
to give us clues of Spring which are
heavenly designed.

Everyone loves a SUN-ny day,
awaiting blossoms to bloom –
to see nature's spray.
Life just wouldn't be right without
natures bouquet
to perfume, to enhance, to delight;
and when at its peak –
what an overwhelming sight.

                            Written Mon., May 22, 2006

ENJOY LIFE'S NUTS

Walnuts, Spanish, Pistachio, Hazel,
Filbert, Brazil, English, Macadamia,
Cashews and Pecans are all fine nuts indeed.
Absolutely good eating
I truly believe.
Different shapes, tastes, coverings and size,
an array of smells with hue-like disguise.
Although different, all tastily
hold recognizable prize.
I usually eat only one kind at a time,
and other times of a mixture
I like to dine.
Once in awhile, I, like you, find one uneatable
and toss it eschew.
We never want to stop eating nuts
or throwing too many away.
Just check them first closely, like I do,
I say.
For so it is with many things in life,
like when you marry a man or a man
takes a wife.
Often things that appear just plain
hunky-dory
are sometimes a "Pandora's Box."
Check first the assortment of people and things,
toss out the worst like old sox's.
Hold on to the Walnuts and Pistachios of life,
savor the odors and taste.
Don't let old Beelzebub steal any of your nuts.
Don't let him spoil
nor non waste.

Written Sat., November 15, 2003 circa 3:00 p.m.
as we drove So. from Indy on I65

THOSE AWFUL NOSEBLEEDS

Often when I was a little girl my nose
would start to bleed.
Whether day or night, at play or classroom,
it seemed to have this need.
It bled most in winter,
that I couldn't understand but I always felt
real bad when the blood just ran and ran.
I soiled so many white pillow cases when it happened
in the night
but Mama never fussed and I know it
was a sight.

Most times when it bled I'd lie on my back,
a cool cloth over my nose,
trying to halt the flow of blood that
menacingly drained – imposed.
One day, when I was around ten years old,
with ball and jacks
I played,
when my nose began a bleeding and nothing
would slow, nor stave.
I then became quite frightened,
tears began to swell
and much to my sad dismay – both nostrils
blazed a trail.

The more it bled
the more I cried,
nothing could calm my fears.
Mama held me gently as she wiped away my tears.
She softly hummed a little tune
which made my soul feel blessed.

I later woke, nose bleeding no more,
Relaxed from nap and rest.
How happy I was
Tho my nose was sore
I wanted to get up and play
but Mama said "YOU'VE HAD THE WORSE
NOSEBLEED EVER,
AND RIGHT HERE ON THIS COUCH
YOU'LL STAY"
I thought to myself "This won't ever
happen again,
I'm just too skinny, and noticeably thin.
My nose feels
irritated, cracked and bruised
and I don't have much blood left to lose.

What a joy and what a blessing that followed that day.
All my nosebleeds ended –
they just went away.
I never had them after that
unless I stumbled, bumped
or received a whack.
I was gladder then glad as I
sang, laughed and whistled with glee
"Thank you Lord Jesus for stopping my nosebleeds;
thank You for touching little me."

Written Fri., April 1, 2005
Non Fiction

KEEP SPARKLING PAM and FAMILY

When children are loved and taught rightly
they become as sparks of living
light in a dark world.
When parents love, teach and discipline,
which now is rare,
children learn to share;
they learn to care and learn to bear in life.

When a home is built,
fastened down and strengthened through the gospel,
brothers and sisters
work, walk, talk, live, love and play together
in their thoughts, words and their deeds;
and the angels hover overhead and
watch in wonder at earth's heavenly seed,
growing, giving and flourishing.

Grateful enthusiasm creates abundance.
Whatever avenue pursued,
particularly the avenue in which one is gifted,
the realization and acknowledgement
of that gift is
shown in the pursuit of the gift.
The soul which seeks, recognizes,
accepts and enjoys
their gift
shares it with the Creator and in using it
He is well pleased.
A child who has grown and become
a light among us is
one Pam Kellar....

She is a spark of living light in a dark world.
Keep sparkling Pam
and Family.
Keep making an illuminated pathway of light
for others to follow.

To all the Kellar Family:
Father Marcel, Mother Lovie,
Sheila, Pam, Jeff, Mark, Gary and wife, Mary,
An outstanding and upright family of Nashville, Tennessee.

Written October 4, 2004

JOHN RICHARD FOULKES

His life is explicitly fragrant with truth.
His thoughts, words and smile
portray perpetual youth.
His glance, handshake and stride are all secure.
He walks with a purpose to faithfully endure.
I've known John now for twenty-three years.
He remains a constant friend to me,
and to all his peers.
He's always the same among the great or small.
He never makes a difference in others,
no nary-a-one – not a'tall.
How my little family loved/loves to
open our door
for John to enter with smiles and hugs galore.
One night when he came
the date had really been mixed-up.
My husband appeared perplexed,
seemed ready to hide, maybe duck..
I needed to change the bed, run the sweeper
and dust
but John had reached Nashville and
called for us.
He was at the Trinity Lane
Shell Station off I65.
He needed Norman to come lead him
to our little family hive.
I squinted at Norman as I pulled out
clean sheets.
LaMont grabbed the sweeper
and Lynnette a dusting fleece.
Norman mumbled
"I'm sorry"

for his mix-up of the date,
quietly exited through the door
for it was already rather late.
Me and the children then hurriedly
put things ACE;
we soon heard the car's motor as it returned
to its place.
And then there was the sound of friendly
shuffling feet
as they walked across the deck to enter
and to greet.
John, in his warm and playful manner
asked
"Should I come in – or leave –
and come back again?"
"Naw," we answered,
"everything's cool,"
we knew the procedure and we
knew the rule –
for our dear friend, John, is a rare
and priceless jewel.
One more thing that needs to be said,
it's about the hats
he wears on his head.
Whether the off-white Cassidy,
the black or the brown;
where his hats are concerned
there's no fooling around.
He's serious about his hats – he never lends
but he's even more serious about his family
and his friends.

From heart to heart!
Written Thurs., November 20, 2003
Non Fiction

AN INCIDENT: A GOOD ENDING

When I turned on Channel 4, NBC TV this morning, Matt Lauer was talking to some Life Guards and the mother of a little boy who had been trapped under a capsized boat. All had thought the worst but found, when righting the vessel to its proper position, the little 10 year old, Darrell Nelson, had held on to the seats of the boat, keeping himself in an air pocket. He had put his sunglasses in his mouth to keep from losing them, and held on for almost two hours. When asked if he was afraid he gave a bit of a puzzled expression and said "No." You could see and hear, and feel he meant what he said. He touched my heart and made me, a mother too, think of my son, Norman LaMont, when he was a little fellow.

I believe Darrell Nelson is going to do great things in his life. God has spared a special little soul.

Thurs., June 10, 2004

And today, August 25, 2005, as I read again this article these words were spun:

Some things happen that make you ask "Why?" Some things happen that make you want to cry. Some things happen that'll make you cringe and set your teeth. Some things happen that are almost beyond belief. Without a doubt little Darrell Nelson asked "Why?" Maybe Darrell even wanted to give-up and cry –but he set his teeth to just hold on tight, and God took over to win his fight. God empowered that they turn the boat, again, upright, hum mmm, hum mm, hum mm mm. MY LORD! MY LORD!

DAILY – CHANGES COME

Awakening with a gleaming sun of each
Majestic new day
My first waking moments crammed full
and with unfeigned thanks – I pray.
I lie so still for it helps me think,
and I breath deep
in-and-out;
sometimes my heart beats wildly
and under my breath I shout….
Whoa ooo oo.
I'll hold my breath till I can't anymore
then slowly let it out.
I'm downright grateful when I've received
A goodly portion of rest
for some dark nights I just can't sleep,
a tossing, turning wretch.
I'll whisper ever so softly,
my thoughts spin round, I bay (yawn).
My senses seem structurally akin to a
mental landing quay.
Dad, now is with me, his bags
he packs each morn.
His inward thoughts seem vivid, few;
he releases, he vents, he storms.
Don't know now, nor really ever knew
what each new day
will bring;
but nevertheless,
whatever comes, I'll find
that song to sing.

Other families and friends
are experiencing too
this same distressing woe
But when it feels too much some days
I know in whom to go.
Help us Lord to bear what we must
beneath the Cross we bow;
the one who bears the malady of mind
remains Your's, Master, Your child.
I often wonder – if it were I – just what my Dad
would do;
and I want to believe I'd hear him say
"Honey, I know it's still you."

> Written Sat., March 7, 2006 as Louisville (74)
> and Penn State (78) played.

Dementia

Many have and many are having to deal with a family member or friend who is suffering with this dreaded condition. For some it is a dilemma more unbearable to deal with than the one who is actually experiencing this affliction. I have prayed for them and their families. I ask, will you pray with me and my little family.

[On November 3, 2012 daddy journeyed to his heavenly home.]

Quay: a structure built parallel to the bank of a
waterway for use as a landing place

I was pondering about how some folk will just leave-you-hanging. You'd been thinking they were on the same page……but when it finally dawns on you that they have another agenda you don't get angry but you do get the picture and will think "Never Mind! Just Never Mind!

NEVER MIND! JUST NEVER MIND!

She asked him, "Would you like to do,
American or Chinese for lunch?"
and waited nearly five minutes
while he coughed, grunted,
stretched and sneezed.
She then asked again –
tho a little reluctant
"You want to have American or Chinese for lunch?
She'd become a wee bit
weary now and a trifle disgusted
but calmly waited while he
hemmed and hawed;
if he couldn't do lunch
she wouldn't bawl.
So with one last effort
toward getting an answer……….
asked
"Will we do brunch, lunch, dinner or supper?"
Starring blankly he nodded nonchalantly
And finally says
"**OH** – I have other plans!
I forgot to tell you.

I have some other things I need to do
so I really won't have time for
either with you.
I'm never really that hungry
and seldom take time to dine.
I – ah, ah aaa…."
When finally he paused
allowing a response of like kind,
she quickly muttered –
Never mind! Just never mind!

                                            Written June 3, 2005

    I found myself writing this little work as I sat in my room on the 6th floor of the Sheraton Hotel in Chattanooga, TN. during the Annual Convention of the Tennessee-Georgia Cemetery Association Convention. My husband, Norman served on the Tennessee board from 1997-2012.

THE TIE – YOUR TIE – MY TIE

It's cloth, sometimes colorful,
different widths,
shape and size.
Some unique!
Some plain and simple!
Some with pattern that defies.
All provide the same effect
when they're place about the neck
and uncomfortable as they may be,
rarely ever will we see
a gentleman lacking one in place
to enhance his neck and face.
'Tis my task, for alas,
if one neglects to don me where requested
then entrance may result divested.
A meager portion of fabric, cloth.
Needful to be elegant, stylish, soft.
The tie! Your tie! My tie!

Written April 23, 2005

CHATTER BOX

I talk, talk, talk!
Prattle, prattle, tattle, tattle,
mouth like a bowl
with a great big ladle.
I'm a gossiper,
I'm a biddy,
I'm a boo,
tell me shoo ooo oo o.

Written September 9, 2003

HAPPY RECOLLECTIONS of MY CHILDHOOD
{1945 – 1952}

When I was a little girl growing-up in Muncie, Indiana I loved to lie in bed beside an open window on a balmy summer night while listening to the sounds of the night. Some were so mysteriously calming and recognizable. Sounds of the insects, cats snarling, dogs barking, the hoot of an owl in the distance, and the whistle of a train passing through the neighborhood. I always wondered about the people who traveled on the trains. Wherever did they come from? Where were they going and what did they do? These were all sounds of pleasantness to me and I'd listen for them like some folk listen to the sound of the sea from a sea-shell. I'd see the flickering of the Fireflies that we called lightening bugs. There were so many of them then but now it seems to be so few. When I'd catch a glimpse of their flash of light my mind would flip back and become flooded with memories of things we kids had done in past summers and I'd be filled with hopes of what new adventures the summer might hold for all the neighborhood gang (pals) in that year. It was me, my big sister, Loretta, my big brother, George, and my little brother, Larry Joe, who later served as a Medic in Vietnam. He received the Bronze Star Medal for saving a fellow soldier's life. From about the age of ten my first cousin, Freda Elaine Merriweather, usually came from Illinois to visit for the summer and together, along with all of the other kids in our neighborhood, we made a lot of smashing great fun.

My big bro., George, although he was a pain in the butt, could make just about anything; from race cars, skate scooters, stilts and more. No one had better leave any thing lying around that had wheels. We were the coolest kids in the neighborhood because he would made these things and we'd share them with the other kids. A lot of them came from other neighborhoods just to see us walking on those stilts. And, boy, was that neat.

I remember pretending I wasn't afraid of night crawlers so my daddy would let me stay up later on some Friday nights to help him find them whenever he was planning to go fishing. They really made my flesh crawl just like they crawled and wiggled about. I'd hold my breath to keep from gagging when I picked them up.I made every effort not to let on how much I disliked doing that. It was a real challenge, much like trying to catch those yucky lightening bugs. I could hardly stand them either but I didn't want the other kids to know because they would laugh at me. Oh but how I loved to watch them light-up. I didn't like putting them in jars either and later I would always let them go. They made me think of tiny, animated neon lights.

We lived at 714 E. Kirby Avenue in the middle of the block right next to the alley. Daddy built a picket fence along the alley side to keep the yard neat but we never painted it white like you would see in ritzy neighborhoods or in the movies.

The night, to me, was like an echo chamber. You could even hear the footsteps of anyone who walked past your house or down the alley. Their feet would shuffle in the gravel and I'd sometimes hum a little tune to match their footsteps. You could always hear the neighbors screen doors slam shut whenever they came home at night or when they went in from sitting on their front porch, or hear their radio softly playing when they had it turnedon. Folks liked the old 78 records and would play them late on Friday nights on those, now ancient, non-stereo, phonographs, and some would be grooving and singing along with the music. There wasn't any such thing as air-conditioning back then. Folks simply pushed their windows up at night and left their front screen door open to let in the fresh night air. You could catch the remaining odors of foods the neighbors had cooked for dinner and that was another plus as you laid in bed for there were some mighty good cooks in the neighborhood. We didn't always have screens on all of the windows so we just had to deal with some of the obnoxious night bugs. There was always a fly or two buzzing around so we'd hang those strips of fly paper from the ceiling lights. I always hoped the flies wouldn't be able to see them in the dark and get stuck to one of them.

Not too many folks had cars, and you knew the sound of just about everyone's in your neighborhood who did. You could tell when they got home from work at night or when they'd leave for work of a morning. Back then folk watched out for their neighbors. When they didn't see anyone stirring about they would check on you. Mama would always go over of a morning, when she hadn't seen or heard Mrs. Carroll moving about, knock on her back door and holler "Hey, how you perking this morning, Florence?" Nowadays lots of folk don't even know whose living next door to them. We had a few that were rather nosy. They always asked a lot of questions, especially whenever we would drive over to Indianapolis on a Sunday to visit mama's Uncle and Aunt, Nathaniel and Verna Scott.

I knew almost every family in our block and nearly everyone in the immediate surrounding blocks. Just to give you some idea: Bobby Lane lived next door and he was a big old scaredy-cat. Mr. Bill and Florence Carroll lived on the other side of the alley. When I was a little tyke, around four, I thought Mrs. Carroll was Mr. Bill's mother. I heard her calling him one day, and trying to be helpful – I ran outside and caught-up to him going down the alley. I asked "Mr. Bill, don't you hear your mother calling you???" he stopped, turned around, and looking at me rather stern like, he said "May Frances, she's not my mother, child, she's my wife." Well, that sure taught me a lesson....two lessons in-fact; never to assume anything for it got me a spanking too.

Mrs. Christine Hill and her son Ronnie lived next to the Carroll's and Mrs. Harding lived next to them. Charles Wright lived across the street right in front of us. Nevada and Nora Lee Anthony lived next door to Charles. The little neighborhood Church of God was on the Southeast corner. Vine Street ran along beside the church. Greg Williams and his brother lived on the opposite corner in the 600 block. They were nice little boys but their folks never let them play with the other kids. Anne Poole lived on the opposite corner on Vine and First Street. Ann was cute as a button. Her parents never let her play with any of the other kids either. Patricia Jefferson, her cousin, lived on the corner of Vine and Seymour Streets. Patricia was sort of mean and would start fights sometimes. I was afraid of her. I invited her to my birthday party when I turned 5 years old. We was playing a game of Jacks on the front porch and Patricia got mad because she wanted the Jacks but it wasn't her turn. She picked up my little glass lantern that mama had given me for my birthday present. It was filled with those delicious Red-Hots that I liked so much and threw it down on our concrete porch. It broke and pieces of glass splattered all over me. Mama was real upset/mad. She checked to see if either of us was cut any where and then she took Patricia home. She had made a nuisance of herself, and mama said "If this child does one more thing I just might have to whip her little behind."

Around this time period Lorna Davis was my best friend. She had 3 sisters, Veta, Sherri Jo and Doris. She lived right behind Patricia on Seymour Street. I really liked her mother, Mrs. Winona, and her dad, Mr. Shelly. He always talked to me like I was a big person and was very nice. The Graham. Mom and daddy, and the David's had all lived in Mounds, IL. before coming to Muncie. The Graham family lived right across the street in front of Lorna. There was Vertis, Lucy, Joanne, John Hart, and Barbara. Mrs. Izetta, their mother, and my mother, Amanda, was never able to agree on matters concerning us kids but they'd always managed to work things out. Every morning Mr. Graham would come out of the house and walk to work. He would return home in the evening and go back into the house. All of us kids would say "Hi Mr. Graham" and he would very dignifiedly answer "hello children." That is all he ever said to us. I don't want to leave out David and Michael, two Caucasian brothers, who lived in the 600 block. They liked to play with all the gang too. I can't remember their last names but I recall David had a crop of red hair and a heap of freckles. They both were real nice. I liked them a lot. Nearly Every summer a young lad by the name of Winfred Henderson would cone from Chicago to visit his Uncle Roy Flowers. Mr. Flowers and his wife (for the life of me I can't remember her name) lived on the corner of Perishing Drive and Seymour Streets. Winfred was a rather handsome young man and all the girls liked him. I liked him too but he was older than I was and treated me like a little girl – which I was. He gave the appearance of being wiser than the rest of us and my older brother, George, didn't like that. The last summer Winfred came the two decided to have a boxing match to see who was the best and all the neighborhood kids gathered in our alley to see the outcome. Well they were going at it pretty rough and was matching blow-for-blow when I decided enough-was-enough. I saw blood and ran in the house to get mama. Both boys had managed to bloody the other's nose and it was just an ugly mess. Mama made them stop and took both inside to wash their faces. She told them never to do anything like that again and to remember they were friends. Also, every summer Ronald and Donald Brandy would come from St. Louis to visit their grandma. She lived on Vine Street right across the street from Patricia. I just can't remember her name. They would know new games and fun things to do. One summer they had learned to do the "Ham Bone." I thought it was the niftiest rhythm I'd ever heard or seen done before and I was determined to learn how to do it too. I got up every morning trying to do the "Ham Bone." I practiced through out the day and into the night. I just about slapped myself silly until bedtime. By the time they left to to go back to St. Louis that summer, my right thigh was so sore, stiff and bruised that I could hardly touch it but I was exuberant! triumphant! for I had learned to do the "Ham Bone" and I was the only kid in the neighborhood who could do it; WOW! HOT DIGGITY DOG!

Gosh, I guess I could go on and on with these happy Recollections of my childhood memories….. These things of pleasantness and fun but I expect I'd be writing for quite a spell so I think I'll just stop here-OK?

Written September 18, 2002
Non Fiction

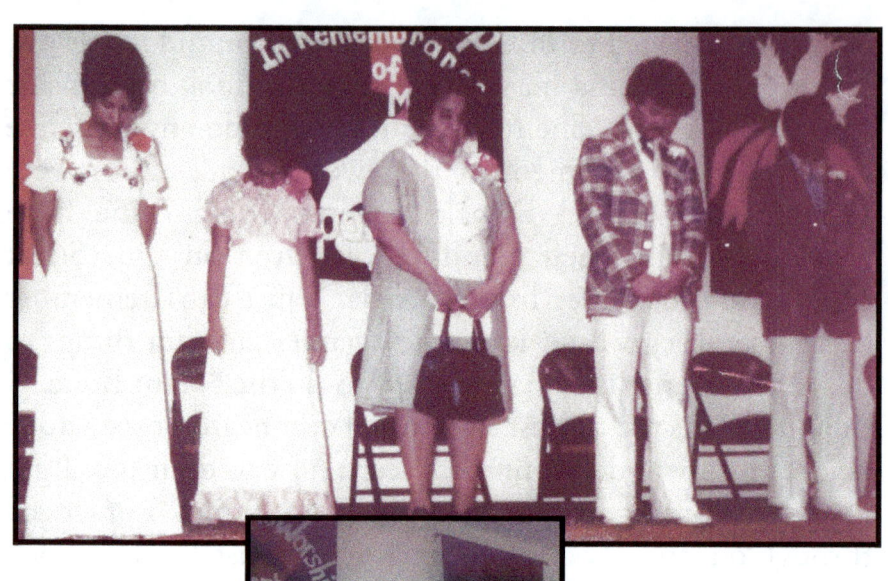

SECOND CHRISTIAN CHURCH
29th & Kenwood
Area 5 Presents

MRS. MAY REED
(And Friends)
In A Musical Recital

Mr. O. B. Manning, Accompanist
Sunday, July 28, 1974 4:30 P.M.

T. Garrott Benjamin, Jr., Pastor
Donation: $2.50

On Thursday, November 11, 2004, Norman and I had driven to Charleston, SC to attend the first combined Regional Assembly of all the Christian Churches (Disciples of Christ) in South Carolina. The Reverend Sotello V. Long, Regional Minister and his lovely wife, Dee, along with everyone else, were excited about this historic occasion. It was held at the First Christian Church in Charleston. Jean Brown, the wife of Bishop Melvin Brown and I sat chatting in the Fellowship Hall that afternoon. Jean began telling me about one of her child-hood experiences. She told me about the time when she was in grade school and her teacher took the class to see a boat. Jean had expected only to look at the boat but when they got there her teacher said they were going to get in the boat and she was terrified. She said "I didn't mean to get in the boat. I only wanted to look at the boat." I made a mental note of her account and later wrote the following poem.

I ONLY WANTED TO LOOK AT THE BOAT

I went thinking we'd only
look at the boat.
Don't like no water no way,
didn't have a mind to sail that day
and teacher only said we would look at the boat.
The water can be pretty, so blue,
every bit
but I don't want nothing at all to do with it.
Now teacher never said we'd be getting in the boat.
No way did I mean to get in ta float.
It was pretty to see and a nice place to be
but I don't like sailing,

just seeing for me.
Don't like floating – just being
and seeing.
Teacher only said we'd look at the boat
getting in the boat
was quite another note
but – **we did get in the boat…**

Written Spring 2005
Non Fiction

Once, when I was a little girl, I bit a moth ball and spit, and spit forever, it seemed. When Mama asked me why I bit it I said, **"I don't know!"** then I thought for a moment – I remembered!.......It looked like a bubble gum ball but when I bit down I got the 'UGH' of my life. There've been a lot of "I-don't-knows" uttered by wee ones.

I DON'T KNOW

Have you ever asked a little child
why did they do a thing?
and the simple answer
"I don't know!" came back
and puzzled expression sprang.
You probably then asked again
and not much more availed.
You really wanted to understand
but the answer
stayed indwelled.
Feeling no intent had been
to mess-up, misplace or destroy, tho the little one
had been told more than once
'DON'T TOUCH'
"this or that
'tis not a toy."
A child wants to feel and touch
the things their eyes may see;
I think to determine
'what in the world a thing could possibly be.'
New sights, sounds, so many things
lying around.

New tastes to test, things to explore
by hand or mouth, on the table,
on the floor.
To be sure saying
"NO!"
won't remain in effect.
The touching and tasting 'me' simply can't
Reject
and for the time being wee
inquisitive little folk
will continue to touch, taste,
feel, sniff, pinch, and poke.

                                    Written Fri., January 13, 2006

I'M SALTY

No, I'm not mad!
Dangerous tho not bad.
Vast room within for some to abide
For I'm mighty lengthy
and mighty wide;
A myriad of space
Many places to hide.
I often leap high,
I'm terribly deep.
Never shallow nor low
but always moving,
tossing to and fro.
Rippling, breakers dashing,
I'm always on the go.
What am I?
What can I be?
I'm buoy and salty
for I am the Sea.

Written Tue., December 7, 2004
Early morning

TOMORROW COMES AGAIN and AGAIN

Tomorrow comes
again and again
but we always call it 'Today.'
Tomorrow comes
again and again
but we manage to keep it at bay.
Tomorrow comes
again and again
but we refuse to receive it that way.
Tomorrow comes
again and again
yet it still is always
"TODAY!"

Written July 27, 2004

END of ME DAY

I'm a-crazy bout me little bathroom,
pretty, perky, pink-n-white.
I enter at end of day
to wash me clean each night.
It's all a-bright and fresh;
a charming space to suds, and comb, and brush.
'Tis lighted well with pleasing smell,
a pleasant way
to complete me day.
I place three rollers atop me crown,
like a child, at my reflection I smile, then frown.
I tie a silk scarf about me head
to catch moisture while showering,
hair neat while in bed.
I shower for the tub drains ever so slow
but generally empties well with the
shower's water flow.
I dry me off with towel so soft,
lotion and powder
then turn the lights off.

To the frig now I go for a bit of a treat.
Purity Vanilla Bean Ice Cream,
tasty, creamy, delicious and sweet.
I dip a small bowl –
settle back in me chair
to savor each scrumptious spoonful,
and watch nightly news air.

A wee bit later I slip off to bed,
sift plans for the morrow – pillow cradles me head.

Night, night, dear Lord,
thank you for this day.

Daily you love me in many and varied way.
I pray you'll again wake me
with golden, rising sun,
giving me yet more time to live, work, dream,
play and have fun.
And one day, Sir, the day we
visibly meet
I'll smile and bow before Thee for I'll then be
all complete.

Written Thurs., October 27, 2005
[While living in Nashville, TN.]

TREE/SQUIRREL/CHIPMUNK and ME, TOO

Tall, sprawling, majestic, leafy Oak and
Walnut trees
standing like soldiers.
One grand, old Oak spreads wide its branches
and shades the flowers
in the little garden me and my sister
planted beneath in the
Spring of 2002.
Old man Oak shades just enough in summer
to allow Sir Sun to peep
between its branches
and spread natures warmth.
When ruddy Autumn begins to appear
nature starts to bare its hues of
bright reds, gold and browns.
Syrupy sap declines and loosey-goosey leaves
begin to fall from the branches
they gripped tightly in summer.
And now
quirky-werky wind sends his blustery gales
to release and send them
swirling and twirling like
popcorn popping in an air popper
till they all have fallen and lay spread
upon the ground.
Squirrel and Chipmunk have a
simply marvelous time as they scamper about
scavenging nuts for Winter;
darting, and chasing one another.

Their animated antics absolutely delight me
as I
watch from the patio doors
or at the kitchen table.
Tiny Chipmunks partake of their patio lunch,
leaving little piles of acorn shells
from their daily snacks –
then skitter away.
I sweep them off as I watch them scurry and play.
A bushy-tailed Squirrel
likes to inspect and dig in my flower pots.
He'll shimmy to the end of a tree limb
and leap onto the railing of the deck,
then climbs down into a pot and
runs around and around inside
like he's on a carnival ride.
My friend, Clarence Pendergrast, named him Hermon.
I don't mind when he plays in the
empty pots but he can be
quite a nuisance when
he digs out my flowers and soil.
Howbeit, unbeknownst to him, he has
helped me
with the planting.
Last year he buried several acorns in a pot I'd left
filled with soil
and this year a little Oak sprouted and began
to grow.
I set it out to give its roots more room.
Hermon came back searching for his nuts
but
finally gave-up.

I wanted to go out and help him as I
watched him work so frantically, scratching
and flinging everywhere
the earthen rug.
I gaze out from atop this sprawling hill
upon this lovely creation adorned with
Oak and Walnut trees
and tiny creatures darting amid acorns
and walnuts dropping.
Bushes green-up, flowers bloom
And I ponder
as I do the things I must do,
And think
"how very small I am too."

                        Written Thurs., October 27, 2005

HE MADE IT BACK HOME

The rider galloped lazily into town –
stopping in front of
the General Store and prepared to dismount.
He swung his right leg over his
horse's backside
but
before his foot barely touched the ground
he was hit and spun around by
a brawny young cowpoke,
medium built of a lad.
He fell to the ground, stunned,
His hat fell from his head.
He was nearly blinded by the force
of the punch that left him sprawled
supine in the dust.
He blinked and moaned as he
shook his head
and frowned.
Baffled at what had just happened
he sat up,
struggled to stand but needed to first
regain his momentum, his balance.
It was then that the young cowpoke
stretched out a large tanned hand
offering him his hat.
The rider squinted as he observed
the outstretched hand,
took his hat and crunched it back down
on his head.
The young cowpoke helped him to stand
and now stood facing him;
his feet planted in an "At-ease" position

as though awaiting the rider to return the punch
but the rider only stood their
staring with a puzzled expression
at the young man's greeting.
Suddenly the cowpoke let loose
an ear-busting
"WHOOP-EE-EEE – WHOOP-EE-EEE"
as he threw his hat
into the air.
"Well I'll be dang" he said,
"dat you Junior?"
"It sure is" answered the rider.
"I reckon I ought ta know you
but ------------ **HEY,**
you must be my
liddle brother-Danny – right?"
"Right!" Danny answered.
"And I ain't so liddle anymoe.
"Dog-gone, Junior!
Pa's been a lookin fer ya
fer months and Ma's done bout
grieved herself
half ta death.
We'ns all thought you were a deadn.
We heard bout what happened
at da Alamo…
We'ens thought
you was dere but when we heard dey'd
only left dem three women
and three chiln alive
to tell what'd happened.
we knowed you t'weren't one of dem
but we'ens jus didn't know ifen you'd

been dere when all da fightin
was a'going on and wondered ifen you'd don got kilt."

"Danny!" interrupted Junior,
"I was aheadin toward da Alamo when I got wind of
a swarm of Mexicans headin dat way
and I didn't have a hankering ta mix it up
wid non of dem dere dudes
so I hightailed it down ta the
Gulp of Mexico."
"Danny, I'a signed up fer a six month stint
on a boat headin for Cuba
and right off it set sail fer Havana.
I been sailing round
in da sea
and it's a mighty heap bigger din Texas.
Done saw a lotta tings I
nevah seed befoe, and done a
lotta tings I nevah did befoe
or evah thought I'd do.
Da good Lord sure made a passel (lot) of
mighty strange lookin
and wonderfer criters dat He went and
put in dat dere sea
and I done seed lots of dem
rite up close like.
Some of dem bout scared me
half ta death.
I jus looked em rite in da eye and
asked da Lord ta "hold on ta dem
till I could git out dey way
and dang goodness – dat's xactly whet He done.
He didn't let go of none of dem critters

and I'm a heaping baholdin ta Him
fer dat.
And I'm mighty glad He didn't let me
go near dat ole Alamo,
although I will say we'ens shore gonna"
"Remember dat Alamo!"
"Shucks Danny, lets git on ta da house
so-ens I can see da look on Ma and Pa's face
when dey sees dat I'm alright.
Dang! Eeee-owe ee eee e!"

Written Fri., October 27, 2006

The Alamo, a Franciscan mission in San Antonio, Texas, and the site of a gallant defense during the Texas war for independence. It was built circa 1722 and consisted of a chapel, convent yard, convent, a hospital building, and plaza, all surrounded by a stout wall. After the disappearance of the Indians from that locality, the mission was abandoned, although after 1793, it was used occasionally as a Fort. In 1836 it was occupied by a force of 150 Texans, commanded by Colonels William B. Travis and James Bowie. David Crockett fought here. Hoping for reinforcements, the garrison remained in the Fort, despite the approaching Mexican general Santa Ana and an army of over 4000. When the Alamo was surrounded and hope of relief had faded, Travis and his men were faced with three alternatives: to surrender, made an attempt at an almost impossible escape, or resist. Knowing that in any event, certain death would be their lot, the Texans chose the last course which would damage and delay the enemy the most. The attack took place on February 23, 1836. Over a 12 day period a small gap had been made in the wall and the Mexicans assaulted in force. They were hurled back twice with heavy losses but penetrated the enclosure on the third attempt. A fierce hand-to-hand battle followed in the chapel. The Texans fought valiantly until but five of their number were left alive. These were captured and killed on Santa Ana's orders. Bowie was shot in his bed where he lay ill. Three women and three children were the only survivors. Remember the Alamo" became the rallying cry of the infuriated Texans who would again engage in battle with Santa Ana at San Jacinto. General Sam Houston lead the Texas troops in this battle which was also fought in 1836. This battle left Santa Ana defeated. This victory resulted in the independence of Texas, and Houston was elected president of the new republic. Nine years after the defeat at the Alamo –Texas became a state. Texas now maintains the Alamo as a revered public monument.

[Universal World Reference Encyclopedia c1968:165-166]

[PRAY TO GOD SUCH BATTLES WILL, ONE DAY, CEASE TO BE.]

WHERE HAVE YOU BEEN IN YOUR DAY DREAMS?

It is a precious thing to just sit
and palaver (talk) with God
in your mind.

If you've never done so
why don't-cha some time.

God is always listening!
HE speaks to us
through our thoughts,
our dreams, and Day Dreams.

HE speaks to us in ways
that may seem unreal –
causing a soul to
take inward, delightful flight, surreal.

Sometimes in our day dreams
we aren't even aware
our thoughts
have abandoned our flesh
and are oblivious to flight,
time of departure
nor aware of exact time of our return.
But experiencing a sense of
a stabilizing presence
when the flight is ended
because
what you've always felt
could never be
has been – has happened.

You've experienced this wonderful sensation
In your day dream
for you maybe, actually have
ascended into
that
Third
Heaven.

Written Sat., September 23, 2006

WHEN WE ONLY HAD the OLD RADIO

You saw in your mind with the radio.
You'd hear with your ears,
you could picture the show.
You'd listen to the music and your thoughts
would flow;
while the instruments and voices
you'd recognize and know.

You'd chuckle and hum as you worked,
or played.
Relaxed as you rested when you sat,
or supine laid.
The radio made you think, use thought,
imagination,
while your mind enjoyed degrees
of maturing maturation.

When we listen with our eyes we may
see
what is **not** said
but it's nice to just listen,
sit,
close your eyes
and lean back your head.

Most listened to the radio before TV.
Took more time for family and friends,
made and had
more time free.
Sat, laughed and talked
and told old stories!

Discussed the world across the sea
but seldom now do you find
such a radio show
and few lend an ear
with a savvy to hear,
to know.

I'll continue to tell me
and remind myself
so I won't forget when we listened,
much, so much,
to the old Radio.

                                              Written February 3, 2005

    I reckon the old radio, along with reading all those Grimm's Fairy Tales and other Fairy Tales is what helped me to have such a fascination for using my imagination, and loving all types of music. I would listen to those old radio programs such as Amos and Andy; My Friend Erma; Bill and Beulah; Inner-Sanctum; Suspense; The Shadow Knows and many others. One station played all the old tunes from the 20's and 30's. I loved those old songs like "Roll A Bowling Ball A Penny A Pitch" How Deep Is The Ocean" "I'll Be Loving You 'ALWAYS'" "Mood Indigo" "My Funny Valentine" "I'll Be Seeing You" "Blue Skies" and so many others. To listen to the nightly news, for me, was an adventure into the unknown. There would be news from all around the world and I'd take flight and go everywhere they mentioned in my imagination. The pinnacle of the weekly news was always shown at the downtown Movies, and seeing and hearing the global news given by the magnetic voice of

Edward R. Merrill, for me was the highlight of being at the movies. And when the globe would spin around and that rooster would crow – Mr. Merrill's voice was resounding as he would say "Spanning the Globe…….." I would be glued to my seat and my eyes fastened to the screen until the newsreel ended; now that, for me, was truly a treat to see people and things happening all over the country and around the world. The other kids would always go to the restroom or the concession stand during the newsreel but I always stayed in my seat.

WILLIAM ARTIS KAPPAN FOX
1917 – 2004

"Well now, who did you say that young fellow was?" Bill, Bill Fox, the young Negro Disciples history major who was accepted at the University of Chicago. He was granted a divinity school scholarship. "Wasn't that around 1940?" Yeh, yeh! "Well now, didn't they refuse to grant Mr. Fox a House Fellowship which would provide him residence and a stipend at the Divinity House?" Hum mm m, yeh, yeh they did but E. C. and Rosa Page Welch provided him housing during his first Quarter. "Well now, did they ever break down and give In?" Yeh, yeh they did. That next year, April 1941, Bill got a call from the Dean himself – Edward Scribner Ames; told him he'd been awarded a House Fellowship. No other Negro Disciple had ever before received a House Fellowship, so this was quite an honor. "Well now, how did the young fellow make out?" Fine, just fine! Fox completed all his studies and received his bachelor of divinity degree in the Spring of 1943. "Un hun, un hun, well sir, I'll say!"

> I was yet unborn when Bill loomed
> forth upon the land,
> and God began revealing His majestic
> pre-woven plan.
> He stood small in stature
> but possessed largeness in thought.
> God imparted keen wisdom,
> both heart and mind He wrought.
> Bill was a listener, a learner for sure!
> He heard the voices instructing
> "Heed the Word, let it guide you, it will
> help you to endure."

Parents, George and Nettie, had raised a
mighty fine young man.
He was bright, he was alert,
firmly on his feet he'd stand.
Hail from Wisconsin but not there would he stay;
matriculated about the country while
learning to make his own way.
He met a lovely young woman who literally
captured his heart.
He married her, Reubena, and a
new life did start.
The world's been made much better from
the impartation of this soul.
He has reaped now the harvest
for heaven was his goal.

Written Mon., October 25, 2004
(My birthday)
Non Fiction

MY ALAMEDA MEMORIES and THOUGHTS

My Alameda memories lie nestled in my heart.
They've been a part of my every day,
they're fastened to my heart.
Many faces are gone on now to their home
beyond the sky
but I know that I will see them again
"in the sweet by-and-by."

For those who yet remain in place
I'll miss the days of seeing your face.
I'll cherish fondly those times of the past;
through thought and memory
they'll linger and last.

Run on Alameda unto the Light and
mountains nigh.
Run on Alameda,
let your works and deeds
stretch far, stretch high.
Run on Alameda,
let nothing hinder your way.
Run on Alameda toward the dawning
of a truly 'New' Day.

Written Sat., January 29, 2005
9:45 A.M.

Norman, my husband, and I, were encouraged to accept the pastorate of Alameda Christian Church (Disciples of Christ) in Nashville, TN. by our then former Pastor, Dr. Robert Hayes Peoples, Light of the World Christian Church, Indianapolis, IN. We served there for 24 years, January 1,

1981– December 31, 2004. We were blessed to move the church from 25th and Alameda Streets to 4006 Ashland City Hwy. where we built a lovely brick edifice, dedicating it to The Lord on Sunday, July 16, 1995. At the request of the Board's Moderator, Sallie Sisson (deceased), I wrote this poem to leave as a legacy to our pastorate.

A CHRISTMAS PARTY INDEED

You're darting and running everywhere,
trying to find that perfect something
to wear.
The office party is going to be a blast
and you're thinking, wondering
just how long it'll last☹
The boss has said he wants everyone
there.
If you have to wear jeans
He! – Doesn't! – Care!
for there's something special he plans to share.
He's been smiling more these
few past days.
We've noticed a change from his
usual ways.
He even held the elevator for
fussy Ms. Podge
and walked straight thru the workroom –
nary a one did he try to dodge.
Said hello right out loud
and gave a little wave to the whole working crowd.
That surely wasn't the boss! said some.
Oh yes! answered a worker with a
clear, cheery sound.
The boss has found Jesus
and no longer feels down.
He went to church with me a few weeks ago.
He accepted Christ as his Savior.
He wants all of you to know.
So that night at the Christmas party
the boss told everyone there

"I went to church!" he said, " a few Sundays ago.
I've never gone often but a friend
asked me to go – so ooo oo oo…
I enjoyed the singing of the fellowship,
the wreath with candles alight.
But when the preacher started speaking
my heart and soul took flight.
The words literally lifted me off the pew.
I knew I loved Jesus!
I knew what to do.

At the invitation my legs felt ever so strong.
I found myself rising,
going forth at the invitational song.
I gave my life to Christ that day.
I gave him total charge
And in my heart I felt as if there'd been lifted
a heavy barge.
Into my life Christ came that day and
in my life He'll always stay.
I know now – this CHRISTmas,
the Savior of mankind.
I'll love, and serve Him forever,
for I've now made JESUS mine."

                            Written Fri. morn., December 17, 2004

IT CAN BE AN ISTHMUS CHRISTMAS

She washed and rinsed, wiped and rubbed
till the cloth was all in shreds.
Swept, mopped and dusted
the rooms
then stripped and remade the beds.
Fresh towels/cloths
to replace the used;
bumped her head tidying the closets
many shoes.

When a tune she loved began to play
she made a few twirls as she
hummed, leaned and swayed.
She danced with the mop as she
thought of days gone by.
For a moment she
was a little girl again and she
began to cry.
But quickly she put those thoughts away –
spun again with the mop
to disperse, defray.
We can have an absolutely
happy Christmas. A coming together
like a human isthmus.
Each of us – an island quite unique
but we must channel together to
form a complete.

Maggie Mai and Ermalene will certainly
be surprised;
not seeing one another in years,
a blessing, I pray, to help open their eyes.

Mama and dad
Split-up when we were kids
and I'm hoping they won't explode,
blow their lids.
Each has blamed the other but I'm
taking the risk.
I've invited them both
and I'll not change my list.
Difficulties,
and differences true,
yet so sad;
but for Christmas this year I'm feeling
lifted and glad.

Children, much like a fertile
strip of land,
connecting
to a larger piece
are often separated
like water from the sand.
And parents! tho apart,
let love continue channeling thru the current
in your hearts.

Lord, let this Christmas resemble a
human isthmus with
love streams flowing fresh and clean.
Cleanse minds and hearts
to prepare anew and sing;
make a joyful noise for Christ, The Messiah,
our Heavenly King.

                        Written Mon., December 11, 2006

TRY LIVING LIFE 'HIS' WAY

The elderly man sat bent and bowed,
his face beheld a faint, but gentle smile,
a genuinely warm smile.
Leaning back, he spoke and said
"I was never able to
understand and accept the
things in my life that I didn't like
and I made it hard for me.
Most of the time I wanted to have my way;
be able to do more and get more –
go places, get the things I wanted and
make my own decisions.
I never liked being told what to do
although I knew down deep inside that I should
listen and do what my parents said
but I just didn't want to
and I made my life and my mother's life hard.
My daddy got tired of talking to me
and mama would always jump in and stick-up for me
even when I was wrong, and
most of the time I was wrong.
I think Missy, my sister, was
a little afraid of me and she would slink
back and just look at me when I'd
done something I had no business doing.
'Mama knew better' but she never chastised me.
She would just say "You go on! I'll talk to you later."
I knew better and it just made me more angry
when she'd act like she didn't
have enough sense to chastise me.
I didn't hold much respect for her because of that.

In a way, I think I was challenging her to chastise me,
to act like she really was my ma,
not my friend.
I'll never forget the day I got three other boys to help me
and we managed to get the back door
open on the neighborhood store.
We carried off four cartons of soda pops.
That was the last straw for daddy.
The owner, Mr. Findlay, saw us just as
we got to the end of the alley
and he went straight to my house and told my daddy.
We hid the soda's in an old vacant house
where we could sneak in-and-out to
get one when we wanted.
When I got home daddy was waiting for me
out in the back yard.
He asked me where I'd been.
I lied and told him "over on the school
playground with some of the other boys."
He said "Where?" I said "I was over at the
school playing baseball with some of the
other boys."
He started taking his belt off and reached for me.
I realized then he must have found out
about our breaking into Mr. Findlay's store
and stealing the soda's.
I tried to run but he had a good holdt
on me and wasn't gonna let me get loose.
That first lick was hard and the second one was
harder. I hollered out for mama and
she came a running out the back door, screaming
with her arms in the air **"WILL, don't ya
be whipping on dat child. He ain't done nothin**

fer ya ta be whipping on him like dat,"
Daddy bellowed back **"He'en a thief, Dora,
he'en a nasty little thief and I'm a gonna
give him a taste of what I shoulda done give him a long
time ago."**
Mama reached out and grabbed the belt and hung on
for dear life. Daddy gave up then, dropped his head
and walked off down the street. He didn't
come back home that night.
When he did come home a couple days later he kissed
my sister, Missy, on the forehead and told
her to help her mother out. Said he was going away.
Said he couldn't stay there no more with a
child that lies and steals and yer ma
won't listen when I try to talk tah her bout him.
Said he loved her and mama,
and me too – but that I jus wouldn't stop doing
things that hurt the family. Told Missy he
would stay in touch and when he found a place
to live that she could come stay with him if she wanted to.
I didn't care if he did leave. I was glad to
see him go. Good riddance, I thought, but I was gonna
be real sorry, real soon.
Mr. Findlay reported everything to the police
and they learned, from the neighbors, that daddy
had tried to whip me bout it and ma had
stopped him. They decided I needed
to go to the Reform School in the
next county. Well I went from bad to worse.
I worried my mama to death and
daddy came back to bury her and take care of Missy.
By then I knew I had really messed up – big time.
but it was too late. When my hearing came up and

the report said something bout me being incorrigible
they decided I just needed to stay there.
During that next year I really got to thinking how much better
it would be at home. I kept thinking bout that talk
ma never got round to having with me
and I think I know what she woulda said.
By the time I got out of that place
I was a changed soul but it didn't change the
fact that ma was dead and gone.
Missy was scared to death
of me and daddy was just broken-down
from all I'd put him through.
One day I decided to walk up to Mr. Findlay's store and
speak to him. He just stared at me as I walked in
but he didn't say nothin.
I mumbled "Hi, Mr. Findlay" and he mumbled back
"Hi Ross! how you been?"
I answered "fairly well, Sir."
"Sir! Did you say Sir?" I answered
"Yes Sir, I did."
Mr. Findlay smiled then, pushed back his hat,
scratched his head
and asked me "Think you need a job, son?"
I was surprised but I answered "Yes Sir, I do.
Yes Sir, I sure do need a job.
Mr. Findlay reset his hat and asked
"Do you think you
could start tomorrow?"
I was so surprised I almost fell over my own feet.
I just stared at him bug eyed for a moment.
"Sir!" I stuttered, "I'll – I'll be here first thing in the
morning.... I'll be awaiting when you get here Sir.

Thank you Sir. You won't be sorry.
I promise! You won't be sorry."
My eyes brimmed over and I felt tears
trickling down my cheeks.

When I got home and told daddy and Missy what
Mr. Findlay had said – they stared at each
other for a moment and then we all
started laughing and crying and a huggin one another.
I believe mama was there too cause I
felt a warm breeze touch my cheek and it sounded
like I could hear her humming her favorite old song
whenever she was troubled bout something
"Deep River."
My life had made a pretty 'deep river'
fah ma and daddy
and fah Missy too
but she's crossed over now into camp ground
where all is peace and I know I'll get to
be with her again
one day cause I done give my life to da Lord.

                                                Written February 1, 2008

Blarney, a city in Ireland that lies Northwest of the city of Cork near to Blarney Castle. The Blarney Stone near the top of the castle, is said to confer on those who kiss it –the peculiar kind of persuasive eloquence alleged to be characteristic of the natives of Ireland. The groves of Ireland are extensive and interesting.

A BLARNEY NEW YEAR IT'S ABOUT TO BE – IT IS!

The Blarney Stone had spun me
completely around,
for to kiss it I had to be turned
up-side down.
I hung, like a swing hangs from a tree,
between walls in a narrow well
but oh how free.
As I hung there alone
about to kiss the Blarney Stone,
filled with curious wholeness of the hour,
my thoughts became infused of peculiar,
impending, persuasive power.
Blarney Stone sets near the top of Blarney Castle
and is thought to possess poignant lift.
I sought to receive such inward, eloquent gift.

And while my heart stood still
I puckered to kiss……….
Feeling the same as I withdrew my lips,
I opened wide my eyes.
I thought "whatever did I miss! Does it take two,
three, four or more tries?"

realizing then – it wasn't the Stone
that would imbue these gifted traits.
It is the "ROCK" of ages
inside my soul that provides the mind's peculiarities, innate.
And so
"A Blarney New Year It's About To Be – It 'tis!"
A blarney New Year to unfold.
A blarney New Year full to behold.

        Written Wed., November 14, 2007

FAMINE OR FEAST OF LIFE

There are youth who feel a need to stray,
to push against the pricks of life
most every single day.
When friends and family advise and chide
they're blatantly pushed away,
for some bear foggy thoughts that mar and scar,
and sway.
Why-or-why won't they listen to the words
their wisdom elders say.

Things are so much different now,
Many changes, strange things and new.
So many choices to make, to pick, to choose, to do.
The accuser's voice is everywhere,
his view seen daily – so strong
and in the minds and hearts of many,
They know their path is wrong.
The accuser won't relinquish;
he'll press till he has won
and when he wins his mission,
its killed another son.
There is one thing only that is sine qua non.
It is the **WORD** of Christ our King
and –That– no one should shun;
for it's essential, providential – the Provider will sustain
the soul who seeks His refuge
and in His **WORD** remain. Amen!

                                                  Written January 9, 2009

THE ISNESS OF LIFE

Loving others, the things you do,
touching those lives that love you too.
And you should love yourself and treat you well.
Tell yourself to laugh, dance, sing, thrive, excel.
Do more than merely work, sleep, eat, exist;
enhance, increase, improve - take risks.
Do more than merely wonder, think or suppose.
Shape for you new thoughts;
define, refine – don't confine
or inflate your woes.
Broaden what you know;
Add substance, value and quality bestow.
Convey to all in godliness
the blessed presence of Christ
The holy blessedness of the
'ISNESS' of life.

Written Mon., December 4, 2006

THE CHILD – A WONDER

It pleases me so to hold a child's tiny hand;
To help teach, to talk, to walk,
to stand.
You feel like a million to see innocent eyes
And enjoy much their laughter
when there's a surprise.
The sparkle and trust you see in their face
makes you thank the Lord
for His love and His grace.
I remember often of being little, quite small.
Grown-ups around me
seemed so big,
so tall.
There was so many things I wanted to know,
so many questions as I started to grow.
I asked questions many, galore –
When in hearing the answer,
yearned to hear more:
Why the sun was so bright and why water was wet?
Why the moon could be seen in the midst of day –yet?
Why the fiery sun would disappear, run away,
But could run so fast he'd return again
Each day.
And isn't that the way little people are!
Bright like the sun, sparkly like a star;
Wordy and changeable, curiosity filled....
The Child – A Wonder
with the Master's seal.

Written Mother's Day
May 10, 2009

I was reading The Tennessean newspaper on August 18, 2009, where Joel M. Learner had written an article which was a special for The Washington Post. It began "We'll give them a garden" –those who gave their lives Sept. 11, 2001. On August 1, 2009, ground was broken for a 15 acre rose garden in Shankville, PA. It is being prepared in which to create a bed of roses for each victim of the attacks. Sue Casey is President/Founder of the organization 'Remember Me Rose Gardens.' These rose gardens will be grown at the site of each of the 3 plane crashes. Shanksville is the site of United Flight 93 and thousands visit there each week. Forty heroes aboard that flight intercepted the hijackers intended crash site.

Seven hybrid roses have been grown and specially named to honor those who perished. One of each will be planted in the rose gardens.

THESE ROSES ARE:

"Firefighter" a red tea rose;
"Soaring Spirits" a cream-pink and yellow striped climbing rose;
"We Salute You" an orange/pink tea rose;
"Forty Heroes" a golden yellow floribunda;
"The Finest" a white tea rose;
"Patriot Dream" a salmon colored shrub rose.
"The Survivors Rose" to be introduced in 2010.

After reading the article, this poem had been planted in my heart for it is things such as this that touches a poets soul, their very being. I took the title from the article.

"WE'LL GIVE THEM A GARDEN"

A plant of the genus Rosa, grows both wild and cultivated;
rare in beauty.
From ancient time a favorite in art and poetry.
What flower could cover more beautifully,
more fragrantly, the earth upon which these souls
perished —died, now grow.
What other flower could guard
with thorn and pinnate leaf.
What other would blossom with color that
eases the heart, the mind's much grief.
The Romans used its petals for medicines;
In modern time exudes/perfume.
The red rose of England, the emblem of
Royalty 'twas displayed bountifully
upon its grounds and in the
House of Lancaster;
While the House of York proudly donned
the brilliant white rose,
perched about like priceless alabaster.

The Rose, state flower first for North Dakota,
New York and Iowa
But now our nation's favored bloom.
The Rose —but none other could manage such a sight;
Such magnificent, budding, beauteous,
impressive showering loom.
Henceforth, those who lie beneath this bed of beauty,
who gave their all beyond life's duty —
in each new year when Spring answers natures call,

These roses, many, will
again and again, break open the earth,
waving boldly, gallantly, SURENE and tall.

Written August 18, 2009

Thank you, Sue Casey,
Your thoughts
"We'll give them a garden"
placed a bud a-growing inside my heart
and a planting of poetry from
God to impart.

TIME IS FLEEING: ONLY NATURE SEEING

Red, yellow, amber leaves
Falling from the spanning trees twill soon be bare.
Brisk, breezy winds, tossing nature about
with teeming care.
Now the leaves keep placidly falling, drifting
Serenely free.
Oh, why can't people too
Like this be – why can't they see?

Many families do now look forward
to a festive Thanksgiving
With joy-filled voices and hearts of thanks-living;
While both the wheat and the tare inhabit the land.
Oh but too much hate and chaos fill mind and hand.
Why won't we embrace harmony, unction?
Why won't we abide together – peacefully function?
The leaves grow side by side.
They never murmur or fuss.
They provide shade and beauty for all of us.
Time is fleeing,
Oh why can't we see?
Why can't we more like nature be?

Written Sat., November 7, 2009

QUAFF DEEPLY the GOOD THINGS of LIFE

Some do much too much for their children
but teach them less and less;
then stand back in wonder
when their lives become a mess.
Teach them good things
teach them truth.
Don't stand, watch, and remain aloof.
Be a part of their every day
And be involved in most every way.
Teach them to quaff the good things,
NOT BAD;
To drink deeply of goodness – be at peace
And be glad.
It's terribly amazing
To see ignorance abound
When the presence of God
Can be seen all around.
It's amazing to watch young men
Let droop their pants
And walk straddle-legged
Their underwear bared to glance.
I watched as three young boys
walked toward me
And each held up their pants.
The three looked downright foolish
As if about to dance.
I was tempted to address them
"Afternoon Ladies"
but of course held my tongue.

I thought, "This is one more reason why
so many disdain, shun."
Young men should be taught to quaff deeply
the good things in life,
Quaff all they can each day.
Be a vessel seeking filling and be filled
To run, To work, to laugh, to play.
Be a vessel overflowing
as you run this race;
Overflowing, quaffing deeply of God's
sweet and wondrous grace.

                          Written Tue., January 12. 2010

POETICALLY SPEAKING

Jessie Brown Pounds was a lot like me.
She wrote stories and poems,
Her pen flowed free.
So many stories, short and sweet.
So much presence of mind to share,
not keep.

Sometimes thoughts awaken you
from sleep.
The magic of words you cannot hold
but outward leap.
Pen, paper, pencil kept always at hand
and when not in place
a writers words
can sift like sand.
Your thoughts need be caught
on paper
no less,
Or some later missing
impute distress.

Ole Jessie
had a mighty way with words
and thought.
In writing she touched and enchanted
One's heart.
When you started to read
the enchantment rose, peaked;
I couldn't stop reading
till the full message
was leaked.

Reading and musing in her writings
I'd find
cascading words became a mental gold mine.
I write for I love arranging words,
reading, writing, sharing verbs.
I love singing too,
for music floods my soul with song.
The two graces God gave to me and
in my heart belong.

Written Sat., March 13, 2010

Jessie Brown Pounds
1861-1921

Jessie wrote 800 hymns. One of my favorites is "I Know that My Redeemer Liveth." She was a novelist, lyricist, poet and editor. She edited four periodicals related to the Stone-Campbell Movement of the Christian Church (Disciples of Christ): Disciple of Christ, The Christian Standard, Christian-Evangelist, and The Christian Century.

THINGS WILL BE OK

Walking thru the streets of life
You become aware of the turmoil,
grief and strife.
But I picture heaven,
Wondrous, peaceful, glowing and serene;
Pleasant atmosphere,
All things fresh and clean.
Not busy and noisy,
minus abstract distractions
But sitting quietly with Jesus,
Filled with total satisfaction.

I can just imagine some things He will say
And the joy we'll experience the whole
Endless Day.
No clocks to awaken,
no cleaning,
No rushing about.
No job to cause worry,
No boss to adhere,
No furniture to dust,
No one to fear.
Only total calm and peace
with my Lord so dear.
And all my friends from life's former
Journey's birth
will join me to celebrate
This beauteous new, new earth.

We'll gaze upon the magnificent,
Tide-less,
Crystal sea.

And be captured and exulted
that this all could truly be.
We'll see this Holy City and enter in to stay.
What a fine and glorious time
For things forever
Will be OKAY.

                                                   Written Sat., July 10, 2010

SEASON OF JOY

With ambient thoughts of what's on the way,
High seasonal joys and festival days,
Thanksgiving and Christmas could just come and stay;
Just last forever and not run away.
At this time of the year
many people smile more and laugh more,
and spread more good cheer.
Church bells ring loud, long resounding peals.
Little children make snow angels
with animated zeal.

And the angels hover close
to view what's going on,
for the children's play is rich,
rare and JOYFULLY strong.
They question
"Why can't this always be,
the joy,
and fun and laughter we now see.
Children's voices filled with glee?
Why can't the human heart but see
how things like this should always be;
More love and harmony in unrestrained joy.
And why can't mankind be
more like children,
see and be without alloy?"

Cease to be steely and enjoy life's total sum.
The Holidays are here,
share now your cheer
With everyone.

Written November 16, 2010

CHERISNA

Cherisna, Cherisna, a sound like music
blowing in the wind,
like a song being sung from deep within.
Cherisna, Cherisna, in her heart she sows –
Seeds of care, seeds of joy,
seeds of faith
and blessings;
Adorned with smiles beneath her crown
But 'tis nary is there shown a frown.
With a light and a twinkle
In her eyes;
An air of enthusiasm,
she speaks, she sighs.
Tones of interest seen and heard,
learning uttered in her words.
Cherisna, Cherisna,
witness and service in your bright presence
is seen and voiced.
Cherisna, Cherisna,
your blessed vision of choice.

Written February 3, 2011

Cherisna is about a sweet, young woman whose parents are of Haitian descent. Cherisna was born in America. She is a seminary graduate of Vanderbilt University, and holds the Master of Divinity degree. She served as an intern Youth Minister at New Covenant Christian Church (Disciples of Christ) during her study at Vanderbilt. The Rev. Dr. Judy Diane Cummings is Senior Pastor. She now serves as

Campus Minister at the historic Bethany College, Bethany, WV, founded by Alexander Campbell in 1840. Prior to this position she served as Campus Minister at the historic Jarvis Christian College at Hawkins, TX. This lilting poem, to me, describes Cherisna. God's church is richly blessed in the work and witness of this individual who labors in His service.

DORY, A TROUBLED CHILD
[A child poem analogy]

The mind, the imagination is a wonder to behold.
The mind, the imagination can be a fantasy to unfold.
The mind, the imagination sometimes wearies the troubled soul.

Dory thought himself a dragon
Dory liked to run and play.
Dory had a little wagon
Dory had not much to say.
Dory didn't like the flames that flowed out from his nose.
Dory poured water on it
Dory thought he'd make it close.
But Dory couldn't put it out
however hard he tried,
Until one day he got so mad
he cried, and cried, and cried.
And then he felt and found no flame,
He wondered and replied
**"I had only to use the Water within me
to stop the flames inside."**

There is a Fountain filled with **LOVE**
That will drive away life's flames.
A love that quenches anger;
A love that removes pain.
And when we cry out for it,
Holy Spirit then 'twill come.
LOVE loves us big, and little.
LOVE loves us all, not some.

Written Mon, May 24, 2011

IN MY HEART

Come laugh,
Come sing,
Come play with me, Jesus.

You see me, Jesus, wherever I go
You are always right here
in my heart.
Whatever I do and
wherever I go
You watch and keep
This I know.

And when morning comes, Jesus,
You bring forth the sun,
Sending light upon all,
Everyone.

Come laugh, and sing
Oh my wonderful King.
Come laugh and sing
In my heart.

Written October 29, 2008

A little poem-song written for the children of
New Covenant Christian Church in Nashville, TN.

But Jesus said, Suffer little children, and forbid them not,
to come unto Me: for of such is the kingdom of heaven.
Matthew 19:14 –KJV

FOR JUST A FEW MOMENTS – RISE ABOVE IT ALL

Should not we live with lifting, lilting
heart and mind.
Spend less ho-humdrum, mediocre,
Dilly-dally time.
Help cause others to look up, think up,
Smile and laugh more.
Just drift away occasionally,
Dream often; why not even snore?

Transcend everydayness that sometimes
Wounds and tears.
Mentally release
gravitational woes and cares.
For just a few moments
Rise and float in thought.
Bring a free, refreshing sense of self
That truly you have sought;
Nothing borrowed, loaned or bought.

Thoughts that release worry and gladdens the soul.
Balmy pleasantness now yours,
Freely behold.
Nothing now to hinder y'all,
For just a few moments, rise above it all.

Written Sat., August 13, 2011

CHOBEY and the GREEN GLASS EYE

Chobey's little scooter was red,
and his nifty bike red, too.
So was his crown, his head,
and his friend's name was Beckie Sue.
One melancholy day he began to sigh.
He pondered briefly
To think of just why,
and then he remembered
The Green Glass Eye.

Beckie Sue had given him this
beautiful green glass sphere.
She said it was magic
but there was nothing to fear.
Chobey jumped and blinked
when he thought about the eye
"Where did she get it" he thought,
"and should he a wish try?"
As he held it and rubbed it and pondered
What to do;
He thought
"Before I wish anything
I'll check first with Beckie Sue."

Beckie Sue laughed
as she threw back her head
"You didn't
really believe me, Chobey,"
she said.
"It's just a big old marble that
belonged to my Dad."

Written Wed., August 17, 2011

CLOTHED FOR WORSHIP

Thank you Almighty and gracious God
in allowing us, Your people,
another moment to bring an offering into
Your Storehouse.
We, the members of the Christian Church in Tennessee
have come 'Clothed for worship.'
Our hearts have been prepared for this hour
with prayer and in various outreach efforts
across the region.
Gathered now in this sanctuary – in thankfulness,
with open hands and glad hearts
we offer these gifts which will assist Door Step Ministry,
poverty, and more.
Continue, O God, to fill and ignite our hearts
with a spirit of clothing ourselves for worship
as we clothe others.
Lead us 'In All Ways' to worship Thee, O Lord.
In Jesus' name we pray.
AMEN.

Written October 2004

Serving on the Tennessee Regional Assembly Planning Committee in 2004, was again a joy. It was held at the First Christian Church in Shelbyville. As always, the committee consisted of church members with various talents. For opening worship on Friday evening, October 16, I shared prayer for the offering, encompassing our assembly theme **"In All Ways Worship God,"** embracing the thought of being 'Clothed for Worship.'

This was my prayer inviting all the assembly to join me in reading. I often think, should we not always clothe ourselves, our minds for worship when we come to His House of Prayer—shouldn't we?

THIS MORNING'S PRAYER

Got up this morning
Bowed down to pray.
I thank you Lord for this brand new day.
Peered out the window
at bird, deer and squirrel.
How they bask in your presence,
enjoying life, sunshine, your world.
I, too, do this Lord
For you make my life whole.
You fill me with anticipation in each
moment to unfold.
I'm lifted up, filled up, pumped up
In Your glow.
I cherish this life you have given me to sow,
So I'll never stop praising, praying,
Never ceasing to grow.
You are my **SUNSHINE, Lord,**
Truly this I know. AMEN.

Written Wed., February 29, 2012
(Leap Year)

THOUGHTS AND CONCERNS

November is when we are to
All vote again.
A day of hope, some doubt
But with determined decision.
Let each one vote with a thoughtful mind,
truly looking at the facts and not
as though blind.
No one need tell another what to do
But just weigh what you know is truth,
What is true.
Daily news sometimes lifts, sometimes confuse
But the children suffer most
when we errantly choose.
More and more the nation is coming apart;
Voices of anger, resentment, bitter retort.
When the WORD is known,
firmly planted in one's heart,
no confusion, worry or fear
will reign or impart.
Let faith, not fear, lead you on that day.
Go and vote in November.
Let truth prevail, I pray.

Written Wed., August 22, 2012

MY TRIBUTE TO
BILLYE PINKSTON BRIDGES
Ordained minister of the Christian Church
(Disciples of Christ)

I'd know her since the 60's
Always helpful, sweet and kind.
You couldn't help but love her;
A hug and smile you'd always find.
Billye, a true servant, had a special way and
Touch,
She was dedicated, loyal, with a laugh
We loved so much.
A Disciple's Disciple with a zeal to learn
And the ability to help others receive
And discern.
Her season was ending,
Getting ready to go.
All seeds had been planted,
Nothing left to plant, to sow.
With a smile on her lips and HIS Light
In her eye,
Billye slipped quietly away.
No more tears to cry.
Now let us run on
for one day we too will see
the face of our dear Savior and
that smile of our Bil lye.

Written Thurs., August 23, 2012

Billye was special and we all loved her dearly. She will be remembered for the dedication and love she put into her work throughout the church. Billye personified the word

"Historian." She served as the Director of Christian Education for Disciples Home Missions from 2003-2012,Christian Church (Disciples of Christ). She was a member of Light of the World Christian Church, Indianapolis, IN. She gave of herself freely and compassionately. We shall miss her warm smile and her contagious, energetic laughter.

TOMORROW DAY

Tomorrow Day, when will it be?
Tomorrow Day, when will we see?
Looking into the heaven's
so far away,
I am very certain
through the veil of time
my heart has glimpsed this ray.
Although said, "Tomorrow never comes"
As I peer into my heart's mind
of azure blue sky,
I sense its presence – some.
Sun winks, shines and blinks as I ask
if this might be true,
then slips behind the clouds
as Sun fondly loves to do.
I'll keep watching, waiting,
For I know surely one day,
Though yet far away,
we'll see HIM coming in the clouds
for it'll then be
Tomorrow Day.

Written Mon., February 18, 2013

Dedicated to the memory of Fannie Mae Braxton
Mother of Dr. Dale Braxton

LITTLE WHISTLER BOY
[This 'twas a dream]

My how they clapped,
Some said, golly, gee.
Others cheered as they called out
"whistle another one, please ee eee."
The wonder they experienced as they
listened to the child;
His little lips pouted and he whistled a long while.
The little lad stood perfectly still.
I felt soothed by the sound
for it was surreal.
Cars slowed to brake
but he just stood still,
whistling so clearly;
My gosh, goodness sake.
More now came running,
they laughed
and smiled with glee
while some began asking
"Who taught you to whistle – you are so wee?"
He then stopped and answered
"I can whistle most anything
Tho I'm only three
For I asked **Jesus** and **HE** said
"YES, you can whistle for Me."

Written Tue., May 28, 2013

My dream made me think of Miles Woods who is a little friend of mine. He is quite a whistler. I like to whistle too. I told Miles "One day he and I should whistle a song together."

He is a fine lad. Earlier this year he gave his life to Christ and was baptized. His mom and dad are Derek and Dr. Cindi Woods-Jones. They are terrific parents. They are members of the New Covenant Christian Church (Disciples of Christ) where the Reverend Dr. Judy D. Cummings is Senior Pastor, Nashville, TN. Dr. Judy is the first woman pastor of this historic church of 154 years.

BETH AND PUPPY

Beth Loved her little puppy
and Puppy loved her too.
She'd laugh and rub Puppy's belly
as children will often do.
One day young bear approached
while Puppy romped the yard.
Little Beth came running fast with fearless,
angry charge.
Puppy whined softly, cuddled safely in Beth's lap,
For Beth had given soundly – bear's nose
an awful whack.
Many years passed,
Puppy now mature.
Beth walked with Puppy daily,
feeling safe and so secure.
But then one day she heard old bear,
she turned in fright to see,
for bear was charging towards her –
Beth had nowhere to flee.
And at that very moment, Puppy leaped into the air
for Puppy smelled the danger, his senses so aware.
Bear reared to grab his mistress
But Puppy blocked bear's path.
Puppy landed firmly on him,
this fight would be his last.
Bear tore, ripped, and slashed
till Puppy he lay still.
Beth ran for safety tho she feared
bear'd hurt, maimed, had killed…..
Dad, with Beth and gun in hand, returned to
Sadly find,
Puppy barely breathing

as he whimpered one last time.
Beth stooped to gather Puppy
with trembling, shaking arms;
What-oh-what would she ever do
Without Puppy's loving charms.

Tears began to flow
as dad reached down to touch.
He whispered "don't be sad, don't cry –
Puppy loved you oh-so-much.
Puppy wouldn't want you forlorn, teary, sad,
but he would be most glad.
He gave his all today for you
for truly Puppy in his doggy mind
sensed you'd saved his life once too.

Written Tue., June 4, 2013

Puppy was a puppy when young bear wandered into his yard and Beth, his mistress, was only protecting her little puppy when she courageously whacked bear on the nose. When Puppy and bear matured the day came when they would encounter one another again. Their animal nature caused remembrance. Bear recalled the the scent of Puppy and Puppy the scent of bear. Would we not all seek to protect a love one? Every species, like the mother bear at the mouth of the cave, when seeing/sensing danger to their own will react through the nature of their being to protect them.

ONE CHILD'S PRAYER

Dear Lord Jesus,
I'm just a child but even tho I'm little
I pray all the while.
I see and hear some gosh awful things;
Mom says this is what hate and
Ignorance brings.
So many are angry,
Guess cause they don't understand.
Their thoughts flow from
others' views
much like opening a can.
People criticize and complain
Saying things they don't really know.
It all boils down to what someone said,
And so....................
Mom says "even tho it's 2013,
many still can't get along."
But I'll never stop praying and hoping
there can one day be,
hearts only filled with Christ like love
for your love, **Jesus**
is the KEY.
AMEN.

                        Written Sat., November 16, 2013

LED TO MANHOOD

Mom taught me good manners,
She showed me so much love.
Dad said, "learn to work with dignity,
Never push and never shove."
Mom said " a man, too, should know how
To wash, cook, and clean."
She said "you take care of yourself, son,
Don't depend on others and
Never, never be mean –
for God is Always watching,
He is with us all our days;
The dreams we hold inside our hearts
Manifest thru words and ways.
Some dreams we dream
Simply fade away.
Still there will be others
To take their place – hooray.
Rise early, don't be lazy, lax, for
"The early bird gets the worm" 'tis true.
And you wouldn't want to miss that wonderful worm
(dream)
God has in store for you."
Hold your dreams in high esteem,
Fashion and shape them well.
Attach God's word to each of them;
Like a sunbeam you'll excel.
So listen to your Mom and Dad,
Cherish their wisdom thought.
Every son needs to be loved, trained, taught
And a Dad and Mom that ought....

Written February 8, 2014

SOMETIMES IT'S NOT THE WORDS BUT THE VIEW

Sometimes it's not the words
But the view.
Sometimes I can't express all the things
I'd yet love to do.
And the hope inside my heart
leads me on to pursue;
No, sometimes it's not the words
But the view
that raptures my soul.
I look around me and find
so much wonder
in things I hear and see,
the rose, the moon and the mighty oak tree.
As I drift thru former thoughts in my mind,
reminiscing and thanking God for
lending me
this earthly time;
I think of all man's hate,
waste and plunder
And I wonder
"what has caused man's failure to learn,
Lead, teach and correct?"
Too, too many young ones lacking a conscious
from this miserable, sad neglect.
Too often a child will practice what they
Hear and see.
Too few walk upright
showing children how to love,
how to be.
Yes, sometimes it's not the words – but the view.

I look at you, you look at me.
What do we feel, what do we see,
how should we walk, talk
oh, how should we be?
For certain we know
LOVE is the Key,
no matter how big, No matter how wee.

Written March 31, 2014

And Jesus said "A new commandment I give unto you, that you love one another; as I have loved you, that ye also love one another. By this shall all men know that ye are My disciples if ye have love for one another.

John 13:34-35

YOU KNOW ALL ABOUT US

YOU know, Lord,
how we live,
How we dance, we work, we play,
We study, we read, we learn,
We write, we listen, we hear,
We see, we touch,
We feel, we smell, we taste, we hunger,
We eat, we thirst, we drink,
We talk, we walk, we skip, we run,
We plant, we harvest;
How we love, and we love this life.
We see, we need, we hurt.
We worry, we sigh, we cry,
We want, we lack.
We enjoy our many life experiences,
Life's many different phases.
We pray – yet still there's times we stray.
We receive each new day
But may forget to simply say
"Thank you, THANK YOU LORD!"
And with each rising sun,
Someone says at the end of day
"There it goes! Everyday goes
And someone goes with it."
So whether young or old,
With joy or woe,
We bid the day farewell.
But all that need be said is
'YOU KNOW, LORD!
YOU KNOW ALL ABOUT IT.'

Written February 4, 2008

HALLELUJAH! CHRIST IS BORN

Why it's time once again when we
Remember His Birth.
Time once again for all heaven and earth
To announce and proclaim
In sweet joyous refrain,
Christ Is Born!

Sing songs of blessed melodies.
Share smiles and mirth and sweet pleasantries.
Let all the world the belfries ring anew;
Christ Is Born for me!
Christ Is Born for you!

While the days grow shorter
And the nights so long,
Work, wait and rest – let your souls be made strong.
Encourage the lonely with kind
Words and song.
Tell again and again
Christ Is Born!

Shout hallelujahs, let His Word be your sword.
Cut out the evil, tie wrong with truth's cord.
Praise the Lord and rejoice,
Christ Is............
Christ Is Born!

[A Poem Song]
Written Friday, Dec. 5, 2003

I WAS JUST THINKING....

As I sat watching the hands on the clock,
Quietly listening to its rhythmic
tick-tock, tick-tock, tick-tock.
Sir Sun shone bright in a clear blue sky,
A beautiful day begun
but why hadn't I.
There were so many things I needed to do
I just didn't know what task to pursue.
I glanced again at the hands on the clock
They were so busy,
they continued –
tick-tock, tick-tock, tick-tock.
I really didn't feel like doing anything at all.
It had been a restless night
And I hadn't slept 'atall.
Again I glanced at the busy little clock,
I watched the minute hand
tick-tock, tick-tock, tick-tock.
I thought, "that little clock looks a lot like me"
Going round and round
I'm just tired and a little diz'zy.
The wash and dusting won't fuss or care
So I think for today
I'll just rest in my chair.

Written Wed., May 6, 2014

SHOO BRO. BLUES

Woke up this morning
Jumped out of bed.
Told ole Bro. Blues
"You get out of my head."
Tired of complaining,
Just laying around
So shoo Bro. Blues,
I'm putting you down.
You've taken my energy,
Synergy, employ.
Taken my initiative,
Left me only alloy.
I'm mixed-up, puzzled and turned around,
So shoo Bro. Blues,
I'm putting you down.
I been singing your blues,
Been feeling so low.
Haven't been out lately,
No place to go.
But come Sunday morning
I'm going back to church,
No more messing around.
So shoo Bro Blues,
I'm putting you down.

Written Thurs., June 12, 2014

I DON'T NEED THESE

I sat down to interview myself
after purchases I'd made.
I frowned and scratched my head
as I looked where there they laid.
I listened to what I had to say
But nothing seemed quite true.
An interview, oh yes, but my words
in disarray.
Isn't that the way it is
Sometimes
when we speak without a thought,
or even why we purchase things
we should ought not have bought.
I asked myself
"did you need these things?"
And of course I really did not.
So I canceled my silly interview
and took back the whole
dear lot.

Written Sun., September 7, 2014

PRAYERFULLY SHARED THOUGHTS

Thanksgiving was thankful,
Christmas was grand.
New Year's Day celebrative;
What today is life's plan?
We pray – more abundance of joy
For all whom we meet.
Abundance of joy
With laughter so sweet.
Abundance in smiles, kisses and love.
Abundance in joys, kindness,
Goodness and hugs.
So don't let nobody/nothing
Hinder your peace,
For Jesus sends angels where
HOPE is released.
Jesus faithfully walks
right by your side;
So just let His presence forever abide;
For in loving hearts
He'll remain and reside.

Written Dec. of 2014

SNOWFLAKE BALLET

I felt I heard great silence
in a maze of swirling
White.
Very large, determined snowflakes,
In hurried billowy flight.
For nearly fifteen minutes-their presence
Full and strong.
I watched this snowflake ballet
Like listening to a song…
(hum mmmm mm mmm)
They seemed to laugh,
twirl, spin and leap
But too soon the ballet ended;
With nary a sound,
No, nary a peep –
Yet I'd heard this gracious
Lilting silence.
It'd touched a deep recess.
No music had been audibly heard
But it moved and touched and blessed.
Mine eyes had seen this silent melody
That left my heart aglow.

The ballet of the snowflakes
Lightened and lifted my soul.
Many were disturbed by this flurried,
White ballet;
Some said
"It's not suppose to snow in April"
(on the 5:00 p.m. news-Chan 4-Nashville, TN).

But I said "Lord, YOU know more than we,
So if you choose to cause snow in April,
It's alright with me.
YOU know when it should rain
And if the wind need blow.
And I just say to those who pout,
It's God's business – SO!"

Written Tues., April 13, 2004

LIFE! LIFE! LIFE!

Life is what you make it and sometimes
We make it hard.
If we follow what the Bible says
We'd be a lot less weary, tired.
The birds chirp their thanksgiving.
The sun rises/sets each day
But mostly we growl and fuss,
wanting things just our way.
Life can be exciting!
"Life is unexpected, unmerited."
Life is unpredictable!
Life is living, learning, loving, giving,
caring, bearing, sharing, receiving,
making choices and more;
Life! Life! Life?

Written Thurs., May 24, 2007

Well, it's time to unhitch your heart,
your thoughts.
It truly touches the heart of a writer
to receive comments.

I'd love to know if you enjoyed
my "Mind Hitching Poetry."
{P.O. Box 7623, Greenwood, IN. 46142}

∧∧

My love for the Body
shines bright in my soul.
It makes my heart sing.
Makes my speech bold.

SEE YA NOW!

"I really enjoyed your book. Thanks for sharing."
>Dr. Freda Elaine Merriweather, Louisville, KY.

"Your poetry, May, is very inspirational. It has caused me to think how I can be more faithful in sharing the writings God has put within my spirit with a larger audience, so please continue being obedient to the Holy Spirit, and bless others with words of encouragement."
>Doris Speaks, Retired Administrative Assistant to Secretary, National Convocation of the Christian Church (Disciples of Christ, 1991-2015. Indianapolis, IN.

"Dear May, Congratulations on your first book of published poems "Come Sail with Me into a Sea of Poetry." I am personally very proud of you. You seem to be very prolific (smile). May God continue to bless you in your every endeavor."
>Mayme C. Garner, Cincinnati, OH.

"I want to congratulate and thank you. Your book is truly an inspirational blessing."
>Mary Ingram, Nashville, TN.

Dear May,
Once again I have been touched and blessed by your beautiful spirit as I read your poems. I indeed "sail with (you) into a sea of poetry." Thank you for the gift of you and for this wonderful book.
>Peter Monroe Morgan, Washington, DC

Dear May,

My wife Shirley bought your poetry book in Indianapolis and we're enjoying it very much.

Clay and Shirley Harrison, Williamsburg, VA.

"Dear May,

At this point we are looking forward to enjoyable reading and re-reading with warm thoughts."

David and Rheba Terrell, Nashville, TN.

Dear May,

Something led me to pick up your book again yesterday and to read for 30 minutes or so from its pages. That break with your gentle and lovely words was just what I needed, and I am grateful.

Mark Miller-McLemore,
Dean, Disciples Divinity House @ Vanderbilt
Assistant Professor of the Practice of Ministry
Vanderbilt Divinity School, Nashville, TN.

These beautiful comments from readers of my first volume of poetry are deeply and gladly appreciated, and will be cherished for all my days. Thank you each one.

www.ingramcontent.com/pod-product-compliance
Lightning Source LLC
LaVergne TN
LVHW021559070426
835507LV00014B/1870